The Inductive Bible Study Handbook

Learn to Read, Observe, Interpret, and Apply the Bible

by Sally Michael

Truth:78

The Inductive Bible Study Handbook—Learn to Read, Observe, Interpret, and Apply the Bible

by Sally Michael

Our vision at Truth78 is that the next generations know, honor, and treasure God, setting their hope in Christ alone, so that they will live as faithful disciples for the glory of God. Our mission is to inspire and equip the church and the home for the comprehensive discipleship of the next generation.

We equip churches and parents by producing curricula for Sunday School, Midweek Bible, Intergenerational, Youth, and Backyard Bible Club settings; vision-casting and training resources (many available free on our website) for both the church and the home; materials and training to help parents in their role in discipling children; and the Fighter Verses™ Bible memory program to encourage the lifelong practice and love of Bible memory.

Published in the United States of America by Truth78.

ISBN: 978-1-952783-54-8

Truth:78

Equipping the Next Generations to Know, Honor, and Treasure God

Truth78.org
info@Truth78.org
(877) 400-1414

Table of Contents

Truth is never determined by looking at God's Word and asking, "What does this mean to me?" Whenever I hear someone talk like that, I'm inclined to ask, "What did the Bible mean before you existed? What does God mean by what He says?" Those are the proper questions to be asking. Truth and meaning are not determined by our intuition, experience, or desire. The true meaning of Scripture—or anything else, for that matter—has already been determined and fixed by the mind of God.

—John MacArthur. *The Truth War: Fighting for Certainty in an Age of Deception*. (Nashville, Tenn.: Thomas Nelson, 2007)

The Process for Understanding Scripture

The best and most appropriate way to begin your study of the Bible is to ask God for understanding.

Pray

Ask God to create in you a receptive and understanding heart.

> *1 Corinthians 2:14—The natural person does not accept the things of the Spirit of God, for they are folly to him, and he is not able to understand them because they are spiritually discerned.*

Below is a helpful acronym from John Piper to guide your prayer before you begin Bible study.

IOUS

Incline my heart to your testimonies.

> *Psalm 119:36—Incline my heart to your testimonies and not to selfish gain!*

Open my eyes to see wondrous things in your Word.

> *Psalm 119:18—Open my eyes, that I may behold wondrous things out of your law.*

Unite my heart to fear your name.

> *Psalm 86:11—Teach me your way, O LORD, that I may walk in your truth; unite my heart to fear your name.*

Satisfy me in the morning with your steadfast love.

> *Psalm 90:14—Satisfy us in the morning with your steadfast love, that we may rejoice and be glad all our days.*

> —John Piper, *When I Don't Desire God: How to Fight for Joy.* (Wheaton, Ill.: Crossway, 2004).

Promise

God has sent the Holy Spirit in Jesus' name to guide and teach us.

John 14:26—But the Helper, the Holy Spirit, whom the Father will send in my name, he will teach you all things and bring to your remembrance all that I have said to you.

Read

Choose a Bible reading plan.

You will find a variety of Bible reading plans on the internet. Choose one that best suits your schedule. Here is a sample of one plan:[1]

January Bible Reading Schedule

Jan. 1	Gen. 1	Matt. 1	Ezra 1	Acts 1
Jan. 2	Gen. 2	Matt. 2	Ezra 2	Acts 2
Jan. 3	Gen. 3	Matt. 3	Ezra 3	Acts 3
Jan. 4	Gen. 4	Matt. 4	Ezra 4	Acts 4
Jan. 5	Gen. 5	Matt. 5	Ezra 5	Acts 5
Jan. 6	Gen. 6	Matt. 6	Ezra 6	Acts 6
Jan. 7	Gen. 7	Matt. 7	Ezra 7	Acts 7
Jan. 8	Gen. 8	Matt. 8	Ezra 8	Acts 8
Jan. 9	Gen. 9-10	Matt. 9	Ezra 9	Acts 9
Jan. 10	Gen. 11	Matt. 10	Ezra 10	Acts 10

Read with paper and pencil ready to record your thoughts and questions.

Read with purpose and expectation to know God more intimately as he has revealed Himself in his Word.

Read through the passage several times, looking for themes and phrases that repeat. Keep the context of the passage in mind as you read.

Choose a regular time and place for Bible reading. It may not seem important at first, but you will discover that finding a regular special time and a regular special place to do your Bible reading can become a motivation to keep that appointment with God and His Word.

---

1   You could also use the reading plan included in Sally Michael's *Meeting God in His Word: A Guide to Bible Reading and Prayer for Children,* a booklet available from Truth78.org.

Observe

What does the passage say?

In *observation,* you will dig deeper and try to discover the author's intended meaning of the text. The following rules will give you the needed tools for effective observation and study of a passage.

Take your time. Write down your observations. This will slow you down and encourage you to think. Writing things down helps you to observe what you might otherwise miss.

John Piper reminds us, *"Writing is a way of seeing that is deeper and sharper than most other ways. We see more when we write than when we just read.*

> *I know not how the light is shed, nor understand this lens. I only know that there are eyes in pencils and in pens."*

Look at the Context

"Context is king!"

The importance of the context of the passage cannot be overstated and should be your first consideration in observation.

1. Study the immediate context—verse, paragraph, chapter.
2. Study the broader context—book, Bible.
3. Read the chapter/book in one sitting many times. (Divide long books into sections; read each section in one sitting.)

Look at the Big Picture

Steps to Seeing a Passage in the Context of the Whole Book:

1. Get the big picture—read the book several times.
2. Divide the book into passages.
3. Label each passage by summarizing the main point.
4. Organize the summaries into an outline.
5. For a more detailed outline, divide the passages into sections.
6. See how the piece fits into the big picture, how the passage fits into the flow of the book.

When Studying a Book or Chapter

Mark Key Words and Phrases

Marking the key words and phrases will help you to recognize the themes of the book or chapter. Mark the key words and phrases with colored pencils or highlighters to help you distinguish them at a glance in the text.[2]

Ask Questions

Develop a habit of asking good questions about the passage and write the answers you find.

Key words and phrases answer theme-defining questions.

Start with the **"5Ws and an H"**

Who? What? When? Where? Why? How?

Here are a few sample questions:

- Who wrote the book, and to whom was it written?
- What was the author's motivation in writing?
- What was he trying to accomplish for his readers?
- When was the book or letter written?

---

2   Adapted from *How To Study Your Bible: Discover the Life-Changing Approach to God's Word* by Kay Arthur (Nashville, Tenn.: Harvest House Publishers, 1994).

- Where was the author living, and where were the readers?
- Why was the book written?
- How were the author's goals in writing to be achieved by the readers?

Identify the Genre *(Genre descriptions follow)*

There are different rules for reading each type of literary form or style. Use the rules for the genre of the passage you have chosen to study (e.g., historical narrative of Genesis or Acts, poetry of Psalms).

Law

Genesis, Exodus, Leviticus, Numbers, Deuteronomy

The law was a covenant between God and man; God pledged blessing and protection, and expected loyalty in return (loyalty was reflected through obedience).

OBSERVE and record the principles that you discover are behind the laws. Some of these principles include:
- Law cannot be separated from its historical context.
- Law must be seen in its theological context.
- Law is a reflection of the character of God and His will.
- Law is a reflection of God's redemptive plan and describes the means by which God could pardon sin.

History—Date, Time, Place, Person...and more!

Old Testament: Joshua, Judges, Ruth, 1 & 2 Samuel, 1 & 2 Kings, 1 & 2 Chronicles, Ezra, Nehemiah, Esther

New Testament: Acts

History can be defined as a factual account or record of actual events. The Bible provides the inspired and historically faithful record of God and His people in the historical books. This record also helps us to know God's character qualities by giving us a chronological narrative of God's mighty deeds on behalf of His chosen people, as well as His dealings with them in covenant.

In the Bible's books of history, we learn about God's glorious attributes and qualities. We get to know the character of God's people and are provided an accounting of genealogies of the families of the nation of Israel, the apportioning of the land inherited by each tribe, and timelines for the judges, kings, prophets, apostles, and the church.

- Read the whole *BOOK* looking for the overall *MESSAGE or THEMES.*
- Read the *WHOLE LIFE* of the character or *EXTENDED HISTORY* of the event.
- Read the *ACTUAL* chapter and chapter *BEFORE and AFTER.*
- Summarize each scene; make a chart if desired.
- Look for important details.
- Look for comparisons and contrasts.
- Make connections.
- Find the conflict and the resolution.

Poetry

Job, Psalms, Proverbs, Ecclesiastes, Song of Solomon

This genre uses the techniques of picturesque language, similes, metaphors, hyperbole, personification, repetition, anthropomorphism, and parallelism.

Simile—using "like" or "as" to make a comparison. (e.g., Proverbs 16:24—"Gracious words are like a honeycomb, sweetness to the soul and health to the body.")

Metaphor—comparing two things using picturesque language, but not using "like" or "as" to make that comparison. (e.g., Proverbs 13:14—"The teaching of the wise is a fountain of life, that one may turn away from the snares of death.")

Hyperbole—language that describes something as better or worse than it really is; describes the seemingly impossible as actual (e.g., Psalm 18:29—"For by you I can run against a troop, and by my God I can leap over a wall" and Psalm 78:27—"he rained meat on them like dust, winged birds like the sand of the seas;").

Personification—representing a thing or idea as a person to create imagery. (e.g., Proverbs 1:20—"Wisdom shouts in the street, in the markets, she raises her voice.")

Anthropomorphism—an interpretation of what is not human or personal in terms of human or personal characteristics: humanization. (e.g., Psalm 34:14—"The eyes of the LORD are toward the righteous and his ears toward their cry.")

Parallelism—repeating words or sentence structure for effect; a common technique used in Hebrew poetry.

The two types of parallelism used most often in Hebrew poetry are:
- *Synonymous Parallelism*
- *Antithetic Parallelism*

Synonymous Parallelism—expressing the same idea; the second line mimics the same idea as the first line using similar terminology or sentence structure.

For example: Proverbs 1:20-21
- *20—Wisdom cries aloud in the street, in the markets she raises her voice;*
- *21—at the head of the noisy streets she cries out; at the entrance of the city gates she speaks.*

Antithetic Parallelism—one idea is contrasted with another.

For example:
- *Proverbs 10:1—A wise son makes a glad father, but a foolish son is a sorrow to his mother.*
- *Luke 16:10—One who is faithful in a very little is also faithful in much, and one who is dishonest in a very little is also dishonest in much.*

Psalms

Different kinds of psalms: lament, thanksgiving, praise, remembrance, celebration, wisdom, trust

Look for balance in the psalms: distress linked with trust; request with appreciation.

Wisdom Books

Job, Proverbs, Ecclesiastes, Song of Solomon

The wisdom books encourage us to live wisely, make godly choices, and understand life from a spiritual perspective. True wisdom is revealed through statements of general truth and through the overall themes of the book.

Avoid reading bits and pieces and missing the overall message. Follow the line of thinking (especially in Job and Ecclesiastes) to avoid misapplying verses.

Prophecy

Major Prophets: Isaiah, Jeremiah (Lamentations), Ezekiel, Daniel

Minor Prophets: Hosea, Joel, Amos, Obadiah, Jonah, Micah, Nahum, Habakkuk, Zephaniah, Haggai, Zechariah, Malachi

New Testament Prophecy: Revelation

Check the chronology and historical background of prophetic books.

Two Types of Prophecy

1. *Forthtelling:*
   - Primarily collections of oracles; read oracles as a unit
   - Prophets saw through three lenses:
     - the immediate
     - the distant
     - and the far distant
   - Preached against idolatry, insincere worship, and injustice
   - Written in poetic form with much imagery; also taught through object lessons (enactment prophecies)
   - Record of visions given to prophets

2. *Foretelling:*
   - Contains literal and symbolic language, imagery, dreams and visions.
   - Symbolism represents future real events.
     - Look for main ideas and, for now, do not focus on detailed chronological accounts of end time happenings (e.g., Revelation reveals Jesus—Seek Jesus).
     - Look for Old Testament allusions.

Gospels

Matthew, Mark, Luke, John

Each of the Gospels is an account of the life of Jesus Christ. These four accounts are similar in many aspects, but each is unique in its focus on the different attributes of Christ's character, position, and authority.

- Notice the intentional selection of incidents to make a point.
  - Look for the author's intent.
  - Look for themes and connections between stories.
- Check parallel passages.
- Note repetitions (they convey theological truth).
- Pay attention to dialogue.

Parables (contained in the Gospels)

Parables use things in the real world to symbolically explain spiritual truth. A parable makes one point.

- Study the immediate context.
- Check for an explanation.
- Discern the main point.
- Omit unimportant, misleading details.
- Identify important details.

Letters or Epistles

Romans; 1 & 2 Corinthians; Galatians; Ephesians; Philippians; Colossians; 1 & 2 Thessalonians; 1 & 2 Timothy; Titus; Philemon; Hebrews; James; 1 & 2 Peter; 1, 2, & 3 John; Jude

Epistles address specific problems in churches. They are not meant to be exhaustive doctrinal statements.

- ○ Observe the historical and literary context.
- ○ Find the connections and trace the arguments.

Discover the context by following the flow of thought in a chapter or book.

The six methods of observation and discovery given below are explained with more detail later in this handbook.

1. **Get the big picture.** Read the book several times to see how the passage fits into the flow of the book.

2. **Divide the book or chapter into passages.** William Mounce defines a passage as: "A passage is all the verses that make up a complete idea."[3]

   Transition Markers—To break the text into passages, look for *transition markers.* Look for transitions in the author's thinking that may not be according to the man-made chapter and section headings, but provide a natural break in the text.

3. **Title each passage** by summarizing the main point. Titles should be brief. Titles should reflect the main idea.

4. **Divide each passage** into sections. Read the passage several times until you begin to see the sections. Each section should be labeled with the main point.

5. **Chart** the clauses and connectors and/or show the structure by mapping the passage or making an outline.

6. **Mark** key words and phrases that will help you determine the theme of the passage. For example, the key word *"love"* in the book of 1 John reveals the theme.

---

3   William D. Mounce. *Greek for the Rest of Us: The Essentials of Biblical Greek.* (Grand Rapids, Mich.: Zondervan, 2003), 57.

Transition Markers

○ **Connectors**—connecting words, including:

Adding	Sequencing	Illustrating	Cause / Effect
and	first, second, third...	for example	because
also	finally	such as	so
as well as	next	for instance	therefore
moreover	meanwhile	in the case of	thus
too	after	as revealed by	consequently
furthermore	then	illustrated by	hence
additionally	subsequently		

Comparing	Qualifying	Contrasting	Emphasizing
similarly	but	whereas	above all
likewise	however	instead of	in particular
as with	although	alternatively	especially
like	unless	otherwise	significantly
equally	except	unlike	indeed
in the same way	apart from	on the other hand	notably
	as long as	conversely	
	if		

○ **Transitional phrases**—some examples are: "after this," "on the next day," "when evening came"

○ **Change of literary genre**—for example, the author changes from a *greeting* to a *prayer*

○ **Change of topic or theme**

○ **Change in setting, time, location, or audience**

○ **Grammatical changes**—for example, changes in *subject, object, pronouns, verb tense, person,* or *number*

○ **Repetition** of a key word, phrase, or concept

○ **Change in key word or repeated theme**

–This list has been adapted from J. Scott Duvall and Daniel J. Hays' *Grasping God's Word: A Hands-On Approach to Reading, Interpreting, and Applying the Bible* (Grand Rapids, Mich.: Zondervan, 2001), 123.

Outline the Book or Chapter

(Check an English grammar book for help.)

Remember: Outlines line up main ideas.

1. *Look* for transition markers. Divide the chapter or the book that you are outlining into passages. These will not necessarily follow the chapter and paragraph sections as they are divided in the Bible text. You are following categories of thoughts.

2. *Determine* the main idea of each passage. These should be stated clearly and concisely in either a sentence or a phrase, and labeled with Roman numerals.

3. *Divide* the passage into sections and write the main idea of each section. These would be subpoints of the main idea of each passage. Subpoints supporting, explaining, or illustrating the main point are indented under the main point and labeled with a capital letter. You must have at least two subpoints.

4. *Continue* placing subpoints under subpoints to make as detailed an outline as you desire.

Sample Outline:

I. Main Point (verses)
   A. Subpoint (verses)
      1. Subpoint (verses)
      2. Subpoint (verses)
   B. Subpoint (verses)
II. Main Point (verses)

Note: If you are outlining a whole book, you will have bigger divisions; if you are outlining a chapter, the divisions will be smaller and the outline will contain more detail. This whole process can be done for a longer passage as well as for a book or chapter.

Research the Historical Context

Note the author's situation, historical setting, customs, and any words or meanings that may need to be studied.

Remember: Do a background check.

For examples of types of resources you could use to do a background check, refer to Resources in the appendix.

When Studying a Passage

Notice grammar—note the parts of speech.

Remember: Grammar matters!

Nouns—person, place, thing, or idea
- Nouns would fit this format: *the* _____ , *many* _____
  - Mark references to God, Jesus, Holy Spirit, gospel.
  - Look up appropriate unfamiliar nouns in a Bible dictionary.

Pronouns—take the place of nouns
- he, they, my, ours, me, it, myself, themselves, whichever, whose, all, anybody, several, someone, who; demonstrative pronouns—that, those

Verbs—show action (*jump, talk*) or state of being (*is*)
- Don't forget about helping verbs like may, might, must, shall, should, will, would, can, could, has, have, had, do, did, does (*I have eaten.*)

Adjectives—describe nouns or pronouns; answer the questions which? what kind of? how many? how much?- Except for demonstrative adjectives like "this" and "that," adjectives can be inserted in the blanks:

the _____ person;

the _____ thing

Adverbs—describe verbs, adjectives or other adverbs;
- answer the questions when? where? why? how? to what extent? (very, not, here, there, too, also, never, always, ever, quite, many words ending in "ly" such as loudly)
  - *The baby cries **loudly**.*
  - *He is **really** tall.*
  - *The baby cries **very loudly**.*

Prepositions—always introduce a phrase
○ A noun or pronoun always comes at the end of the prepositional phrase; show how two words or ideas are related—about, according to, across, behind, before, between, during, except, for, from, in place of, inside, into, near, on account of, through, up, until, with.
○ A prepositional phrase functions either as an adjective or an adverb.

Independent Connectors—join two equal things
○ and, also, but, or, nor, yet, further, furthermore, however, likewise, moreover, on the contrary, on the other hand, rather
- **[for]**—Sometimes the word *for* at the beginning of a sentence can simply express continuation and therefore function as an independent connector. When the word *for* is found within a sentence it often functions as a dependent connector to express ground/reason. Therefore, we have included *for* in both lists. While *for* is grammatically a *coordinating conjunction,* it is often used within sentences to express a subordinate idea.

Dependent Connectors—although, as, as if, as long as, as soon as, because, even as, even though, except, for, if, in order that, in that, just as, nevertheless, provided [that], since, so, so that, therefore, though, unless, when, whenever, where, wherever, while [for]—(See note above)

Note: When looking at LOGICAL RELATIONSHIPS rather than grammatical relationships, you will find that some dependent connectors (such as "in order that" and "therefore") may introduce main ideas. Think very carefully and make an interpretative judgment. Remember that interpretation is an art as well as a science.

Observe unusual words or phrases, emphatic words (words used for emphasis—e.g., truly). Mark emphatics with an exclamation point.

Mark time references—then, after, until, when

Coordinating Conjunctions

- ° Take note of coordinating conjunctions; they join two equal things.
- ° An easy way to remember the coordinating conjunctions is with the acrostic **"FANBOYS"**:
    - **For**—means "because"; gives a reason
    - **And**—joins two similar ideas
    - **Nor**—joins two negative alternatives
    - **But**—joins two contrasting ideas
    - **Or**—joins two alternative ideas
    - **Yet**—means "but"
    - **So**—indicates that the second idea is a result of the first idea

Identify Literary Techniques

Remember: Take a peek at technique.

- ° **Repetition** of key words and ideas
- ° **Lists**—number items; note groupings and progression
- ° **Rhetorical questions**—an answer is not expected; answer is obvious; used to make a stronger statement of truth
- ° **Emotional words and tone**
- ° **Figurative language**—doesn't mean exactly what it says

Remember: Some words paint pictures of truth!

1. Assume that the language is literal (that it means exactly what it says and should be taken at face value) except in the following instances:
    - ° The statement would be absurd or illogical if it were taken literally (e.g., trees clapping is completely illogical; trees can't clap).
    - ° The context demonstrates that the language is figurative. (The Bible is not a bunch of one-liners strung together.)

○ Taking the text literally would contradict a clearer statement of truth in the Bible.

2. The author's and the original readers' intent must determine whether a passage should be taken literally or figuratively.

Simile—compares two unlike things using "like" or "as"

Metaphor—compares two unlike things using the verb "to be"

Personification—gives human qualities to non-human things or ideas

Irony—says one thing but means another (usually the opposite)

Hyperbole—exaggerates to make a point

Look for key words—words that have significant importance in the text, that cannot be removed from it. Mark each key word differently.

Follow the Flow of Thought Within a Passage

Remember: Connect the thoughts!

Find the **connectors** and isolate the **clauses**:

1. Find all the independent connectors. Mark these with a red square. Independent connectors are used as connecting words at the beginning of independent clauses or within clauses.

2. Find the dependent connectors. Circle these in red.

3. Put prepositional phrases in parentheses.

4. Bracket all the clauses. Keep the independent connector separate from the independent clause when it is joining two clauses; keep the independent connector within the clause when it is joining two words or phrases. Keep the dependent connector within the dependent clause.

5. Label the independent (I) and dependent (D) clauses.

○ Independent clause: group of words containing a subject and a verb expressing a complete thought; can stand alone as a sentence

- Dependent clause: group of words that contains a subject and a verb BUT does not express a complete thought; cannot stand alone as a sentence

    Example: *Colossians 3:1*

    Dependent clause: *If then you have been raised with Christ,*

    Independent clause: *seek the things that are above, where Christ is, seated at the right hand of God.*

6. Make a **Flow of Thought Chart** and/or **Map** the passage.

Flow of Thought Chart:

Connectors	Independent Clauses	Dependent Clauses	Purpose for Connectors
Add rows as needed			

Mapping—Rewrite the passage using the following rules:

1. **Make a Mechanical Layout:** Draw a left margin line on your paper. Keeping the words in order:
   - Write the **Independent Clauses** (can stand alone as a complete sentence) at the left-hand margin. Include the subject, verb, and word or phrase indicating the direct object.
   - Write the **Dependent Clauses** (cannot stand alone as a complete sentence) or modifying phrases on the next line under the word they describe. (Modifiers include adverbial phrases and clauses and relative clauses. These phrases or clauses may also include modifiers that would be indented on the next line, so that the final product might appear terraced.)
   - Write the **Connecting Words** above the line or joined to modified phrases or clauses with bracketing lines.

2. **Label the Connections:** Determine the logical connection between the clauses or phrases and write the connection to the left of the margin line.

Example: 6:19	**Do not**	lay up for yourselves treasures on earth
	AND	⌐ where moth and rust destroy ⌐ where thieves break in and steal
Contrast 6:20	**BUT**	lay up for yourselves treasures in heaven
	AND	⌐ where neither moth nor rust destroys ⌐ where thieves do not break in and steal
Reason 6:21	**FOR**	where your treasure is there will your heart be also

3. **Find the Main Point:** Star the main point of the passage using the logical relationships as a guide.

4. **Summarize:** Summarize the logic of the passage in your own words.

—This technique and the chart below are extensions of the mechanical layout explained in Robertson McQuilkin's *Understanding and Applying the Bible* (Chicago: Moody Press, 1992), 145-147.

Make Logical Connections: Understand the connections between clauses or statements (propositions).

Time (T): (answers the question—When?) after, as, before, now, then, until, when, while, during, meanwhile, then, next

> John 11:5-6—*Now Jesus loved Martha and her sister and Lazarus. So, when he heard that Lazarus was ill, he stayed two days longer in the place where he was.*

Place (Pl): (answers the question—Where?) where, wherever, in

> John 7:1—*After this Jesus went about in Galilee. He would not go about in Judea, because the Jews were seeking to kill him.*

Continuation or Series (S): (sequence of events, things or ideas; each statement contributes to the overall concept) and, or, either... or, neither...nor, like, also, in addition, also, furthermore, moreover, in addition

2 Peter 1:5-7—*For this very reason make every effort to supplement your faith with virtue, and virtue with knowledge, and knowledge with self-control, and self-control with steadfastness, and steadfastness with godliness, and godliness with brotherly affection, and brotherly affection with love.*

Progression (Pro): (answers the question—Then what? statements build toward a climax)

Romans 8:38-39—*For I am sure that neither death nor life, nor angels nor rulers, nor things present nor things to come, nor powers, not height nor depth, nor anything else in all creation, will be able to separate us from the love of God in Christ Jesus our Lord.*

Contrast (Con): but, nevertheless, however, yet, otherwise, whereas, yet, on the contrary, on the other hand

Psalm 73:26—*My flesh and my heart may fail, but God is the strength of my heart and my portion forever.*

Comparison (Cp): (answers the question—Like what?) also, as, as...so, likewise, so also, moreover, than

Ephesians 5:25—*Husbands, love your wives, as Christ loved the church and gave himself up for her,...*

Explanation and Clarification (Ex): includes summaries, restatements, and illustrations

1 Corinthians 1:26—*For consider your calling, brothers: not many of you were wise according to worldly standards, not many were powerful, not many were of noble birth.*

Purpose (Pur): (answers the question—Why?; tells why an action takes place) so that, in order to, that, to

1 John 1:4—*And we are writing these things so that our joy may be complete.*

Reason or Cause or Ground (G): (draw conclusions from prior statements or state the basis for conclusions; reason can come before or after statement) for, since, because, therefore, thus, so, then, consequently, for this reason

Romans 5:1—*Therefore, since we have been justified by faith, we have peace with God through our Lord Jesus Christ.*

Hebrews 10:23—*Let us hold fast the confession of our hope without wavering, for he who promised is faithful.*

Cause and Effect (C/E): (one statement describes what happened or what is true; the second explains how or why it came about—e.g., Since it rained, we had to cancel the softball game.) since, then, consequently, and

Mark 4:39—*And he awoke and rebuked the wind and said to the sea, "Peace! Be still!" And the wind ceased, and there was a great calm.*

Concession (Css): (answers the question "In spite of what?"; concedes that one thing is true even though we have reason to expect another— e.g., We had a wonderful picnic, even though it rained) although, even though, nevertheless, in spite of, yet, nonetheless

Hebrews 5:8—*Although he was a son, he learned obedience through what he suffered.*

Condition or Possibility (Poss): if, if...then

2 Corinthians 5:17a—*Therefore, if anyone is in Christ, he is a new creation...*

Result (R): so that, so, then

1 Peter 1:6-7—*In this you rejoice, though now for a little while, if necessary, you have been grieved by various trials, ⁷so that the tested genuineness of your faith—more precious than gold that perishes though it is tested by fire...*

Note: Connections are not automatic; check the context. Not every logical connection uses a connecting word as a signal.

–Information adapted from Robertson McQuilkin's *Understanding and Applying the Bible.* (Chicago: Moody Press,1992), 142; and from Daniel Doriani's *Getting the Message.* (Phillipsburg, N.J.: P&R Pub., 1996), 89-91.

Find the Main Point

- The main point will usually be in an independent clause, not a dependent clause.

  John 20:21b—*As the Father has sent me, even so **I am sending you**.*

- Usually, if there is a command in the sentences, the main point is the command.

  Matthew 10:19—*When they deliver you over, **do not be anxious** how you are to speak or what you are to say, for what you are to say will be given to you in that hour.*

  Ephesians 6:14-15—**Stand** *therefore, having fastened on the belt of truth, and having put on the breastplate of righteousness, [15]and, as shoes for your feet, having put on the readiness given by the gospel of peace.*

- There is an exception to these rules: If there is a phrase that shows purpose or result, often the main point will be in that clause instead, even if it is a dependent clause. Words like "that," "so that," and "in order that" can signal a purpose or a result.

  John 15:17—*"These things I command you, so that **you will love one another**."*

  Revelation 3:11—*I am coming soon. Hold fast what you have, so that **no one may seize your crown**.*

- If there is a contrast between something positive and something negative, often the main point will fall in the positive phrase.

  1 Timothy 6:11—*But as for you, O man of God, flee these things. **Pursue righteousness, godliness, faith, love, steadfastness, gentleness**.*

  Titus 1:15—**To the pure, all things are pure,** *but to the defiled and unbelieving, nothing is pure; but both their minds and their consciences are defiled.*

1 Thessalonians 5:15—*See that no one repays anyone evil for evil, but* **always seek to do good to one another and to everyone.**

○ The word "therefore" often signals the conclusion of the reasoning that comes before it, and "therefore" often introduces the main point ("so" can also show a conclusion).

1 Corinthians 6:19-20—*Or do you not know that your body is a temple of the Holy Spirit within you, whom you have from God? You are not your own,* ²⁰*for you were bought with a price.* **So glorify God in your body.**

2 Peter 3:13-14—*But according to his promise we are waiting for new heavens and a new earth in which righteousness dwells.* ¹⁴*Therefore, beloved, since you are waiting for these,* **be diligent to be found by him without spot or blemish, and at peace.**

○ When finding the main point in a longer section of Scripture, first try to find the main point of each sentence of the passage.

○ Once you have isolated all the main points in a passage, then figure out which main points are supporting statements for other main points. Try to do so by starting with the first main point and figure out how it relates to the next one. Work your way down the passage that way. Try to find the key main point that does not seem to be supporting other main points.

Finding the main point is subjective—even scholars disagree on this sometimes. So just do your best and check your work against a couple of experts if you're unsure. Also, note that an extended passage of Scripture might not have only one main point but rather a sequence of main points, as in the epistles of John and James.

Classify the statements. For example:

○ Promises
○ Commands or Instructions (to do or not to do something)
○ Warnings

Study the Context: Remember "CONTEXT IS KING!"

- ° **Study** the immediate context: verse, paragraph, chapter, book.
- ° **Study** the broader context: book, Bible.
- ° **Read** the chapter/book in one sitting many times. (Divide long books into sections. Read each section in one sitting.)

Review the Steps to Seeing the Passage in the Context of the Whole Book:

1. Get the big picture. Read the book several times.
2. Divide the book into passages.
3. Label each passage by summarizing the main point.
4. Organize the summaries into an outline.
5. For a more detailed outline, divide the passages into sections.
6. See how the piece fits into the big picture, how the passage fits into the flow of the book.

Interpret

What does the passage mean?

Main Principle of Inductive Bible Study Interpretation:

Use the Bible to interpret the Bible

Principles of Interpretation

1. **Look at the verse in context.**

   Example: *1 Corinthians 1:14—I thank God that I baptized none of you except Crispus and Gaius,*

   This statement makes sense when looked at in the context of 1 Corinthians 1:10-15. Paul is concerned that the Corinthians were identifying with a leader rather than with Christ.

2. **Look for the author's intended meaning of the text.**

   Example: *1 Corinthians 1:17—For Christ did not send me to baptize but to preach the gospel, and not with words of eloquent wisdom, lest the cross of Christ be emptied of its power.*

   The church in Corinth was listening to worldly wisdom, as well as fighting over which leader baptized them. Paul is not against baptism and wisdom. He is making a statement about the supremacy of the gospel.

3. **Notice figurative language.**

   Example: *Psalm 98:8—Let the rivers clap their hands; let the hills sing for joy together.*

4. **Interpret the biblical text literally unless there is a reason not to do so.**

   Example: *John 6:51a—"I am the living bread that came down from heaven. If anyone eats of this bread, he will live forever."*

   To take this literally would be to think that Jesus is proposing cannibalism. "Eat this bread" is a reference to believing in Jesus.

5. **Remember that the Bible often uses ordinary, everyday language, not technical language.**

   Example: The reference in Luke 8:43 to the woman who had spent "all her living on physicians" does not mean that she spent every single coin, but is a general statement intending to show that she spent a great deal of money.

6. **Earlier texts should be interpreted in light of later revelation.**

   Example: The Old Testament texts regarding animal sacrifices are no longer the practice of the Christian, because New Testament texts show Jesus as the fulfillment of the Old Testament sacrificial system. Jesus is a better and permanent sacrifice for sin.

7. **Doctrine should be based on clear Scripture passages.**

   Example: The doctrine of salvation is not based on the story of the rich young ruler (where Jesus asks the young man to give up that which is holding him back from the Kingdom—"sell all you have"), but on a clear teaching like Ephesians 2:8-9.

8. **Define unclear or key words in light of the biblical usage of the word.** (See: e-sword.net)

9. **Unclear passages should be interpreted in light of clear passages.**

   Example: *Matthew 7:8a— ...everyone who asks receives—* needs to be interpreted in light of *1 John 5:14b...that if we ask anything according to his will he hears us.*

–Adapted in part from David Bryant's *Writing and Leading Bible Studies*, published in 2006.

Discern the Biblical Principle in a text:

- **Biblical Principles** are applicable to all people in all cultures at all times.
- **Biblical Principles** should be verified by other Scriptures.

  Example: *Matthew 5:13-16:* True Christians overflow with good works as a testimony to the goodness of God.

Look at the passage from the **FALLEN-CONDITION FOCUS:** through the lens of the doctrine of man—the fall and sin. When you see this, you will see that every part of Scripture shows how Jesus is the answer to the sin problem.

–Daniel M. Doriani's Getting the Message: A Plan for Interpreting and Applying the Bible. (Phillipsburg, N.J.: P&R Publishing, 1996), 171.

Some questions to ask:

- What does this passage tell me about *human nature?*
- What does this passage tell me about *the fall or the nature of sin?*
- What does this passage tell me about *the past state of the world?*
- What does this passage tell me about *the current state of the world?*

Look at the passage from the **REDEMPTIVE-HISTORICAL FOCUS:** through the lens of the doctrine of God—His grace and His sovereignty. When you see this, you will see that every part of Scripture shows the need for a Savior; Jesus' work of salvation, and the result of His salvation; and the perseverance, sanctification, and glorification of the believer.

–Daniel M. Doriani's Getting the Message: A Plan for Interpreting and Applying the Bible (Phillipsburg, N.J.: P&R Publishing, 1996), 171.

Some questions to ask:

- What does this passage tell me about *God's redemption?*
- What does this passage tell me about *Jesus' death and resurrection?*

- What does this passage tell me about *God's sovereignty and grace?*

Remember: History is "HIS story!"

Check Verses Noted as Cross References

Look for:
- Parallel Passages
- Similar Ideas
- Contrasting Ideas
- Context

  Example: Jesus' statement in Luke 14:26 that a person cannot be His disciple if that person "does not hate his own father and mother..." must be interpreted in light of this clarifying passage:

  Matthew 10:37a—"Whoever loves father or mother more than me is not worthy of me..."

As a Last (but important) Step in Interpretation:
Check with an Expert
- Compare your understanding of a text with that of reliable Bible scholars.
- See Resources in the appendix for a list of study Bibles, Bible concordances, commentaries, and Bible dictionaries.

Apply

How does God want me to respond to the passage?

Application is "personalizing" Scripture.

Application should be realistic.
- **Method 1:** Personalize the principle—make a specific application of the biblical principle to your life
- **Method 2:** Examine the passage to find application responses.

Personalize the principle using life-application questions:
- What does this passage mean for me?
- How does this passage apply to my life?
- How does it apply to my family, my friendships and other relationships, my life at school, at home, at church, etc?
- What changes do I need to make? Is there something I need to start doing or to stop doing?
- How will I make these changes? (What is my plan?)
- How should I pray about this truth?
- What verse/s should I memorize?
- What illustration or word picture will help me remember what I've read?
- Who will hold me accountable?

Ask these questions and write your answers:

What should I *think*?	
What should I *be*?	
What should I *do*?	

What action do I need to take?

Is there a...

Command to obey	Character quality to imitate
Promise to hold on to	Prayer topic to focus on
Example to follow	Something to be thankful for
Example to avoid	Temptation to resist
Warning to heed	Error to avoid
Advice to follow	Perspective to ponder
Attitude to change	Priority to establish
Truth to believe	Tactic to employ
Teaching to put into practice	Verse to memorize
Sin to repent of and turn from	Something to teach or tell others

Appendix

Resources

Websites

- Bible Gateway—biblegateway.com
- Blue Letter Bible—blueletterbible.org
- Bible.org—bible.org
- Desiring God—desiringGod.org (search by text for helpful commentary on Scripture passages)
- E-Sword—e-sword.net (Bible software free download)

Bibles

- *English Standard Version* (with cross references)
- *ESV Study Bible*
- *The New Inductive Study Bible* (ESV)
- *ESV Reformation Study Bible* (Ligonier Ministries)
- *ESV, MacArthur Study Bible*
- *Key Word Study Bible* by Zodhiates
- *The Hebrew-Greek Key Study Bible* by Zodhiates

Commentaries

- *New Bible Commentary* (The New Bible Set) (InterVarsity Press/Eerdmans, 1994)
- *New International Bible Commentary* (Zondervan, 1986)
- *Evangelical Commentary on the Bible* by Walter Elwell (Baker, 1989)
- *NIV Compact Bible Commentary* by John Sailmaner (Hodder and Stoughton,1994)
- *Matthew Henry's Commentary on the Whole Bible* (free online)

Bible Dictionaries

- *International Standard Bible Encyclopedia* (Eerdmans)
- *New Bible Dictionary* (InterVarsity Press)
- *Eerdman's Bible Dictionary* (Eerdmans)

Books

- *Grasping God's Word: A Hands-On Approach to Reading, Interpreting, and Applying the Bible* by J. Scott Duvall and J. Daniel Hays
- *Holman Book of Biblical Charts, Maps, & Reconstructions* by Marsha A. Ellis Smith
- *How to Read the Bible for All Its Worth* by Gordon Fee and Douglas Stewart
- *How to Study the Bible and Enjoy It* by Skip Heitzig
- *How To Study Your Bible* by Kay Arthur
- *Living By the Book: The Art and Science of Reading the Bible* by Howard Hendricks and William Hendricks
- Precept Inductive Bible Studies by Kay Arthur

My Codes

Fill in your choice of symbols or markings for the following key words: *(Add other key words and markings as desired.)*

Jesus		blood		nouns	
God		love		pronouns	
Holy Spirit		witness		verbs: past present future	
man		sin			
gospel		grace		adjectives *"add"* to nouns	
life		belief/faith		adverbs *"add"* to verbs	
death		flesh		prepositional phrases	
law		curse		independent connectors mark with an **I**	
references to time		salvation		dependent connectors mark with a **D**	
Groups of people (e.g., Israelites)					

Grammar Marking Guide

nouns and **pronouns**—write the noun that the pronoun replaces above the pronoun:

> God
> **He**

verbs   *past*—brown;   *present*—green;   *future*—blue

adjectives and **adverbs**—draw an arrow to the words they modify

[clause] write an **"I"** above independent clauses; write a **"D"** above dependent clauses

coordinating conjunctions

other connecting words

{ keep coordinating conjunctions **outside** the clause when *connecting clauses*; **inside** the clause when *connecting words or phrases*

(prepositional phrase)

Marking Sample:
Matthew 6:19-21

I
[Do not lay up for yourselves treasures on earth],

D
(where)moth and rust destroy] and

D
(where)thieves break in and steal], ²⁰but

I
[lay up for yourselves treasures in heaven],

D
(where (neither) moth (nor) rust destroys] and

D
(where)thieves do not break in and steal].

D
²¹For (where)your treasure is],

I
(there)your heart will be also].

Notes

Truth:78

Truth78 is a vision-oriented ministry for the next generations—that they may know, honor, and treasure God, setting their hope in Christ alone, so that they will live as faithful disciples for the glory of God.

Our mission is to inspire and equip the church and the home for the comprehensive discipleship of the next generation.

We are committed to developing resources and training that are God-centered, Bible-saturated, gospel-focused, Christ-exalting, Spirit-dependent, doctrinally grounded, and discipleship-oriented.

Resources and Training Materials

Truth78 offers the following categories of resources and training materials to equip the body of Christ and Christian parents:

Curriculum

We publish materials designed for formal Bible instruction. The scope and sequence of these materials reflects our commitment to teach children and youth the whole counsel of God over the course of their education. Materials include curricula for Sunday School, Midweek Bible programs, Backyard Bible Clubs or Vacation Bible School, and Intergenerational studies. Most of these materials can easily be adapted for use in Christian schools and education in the home.

Vision-Casting and Training

We offer a wide variety of booklets, video and audio seminars, articles, and other practical training resources that highlight and further expound our vision, mission, and values, as well as our educational philosophy and methodology. Many of these resources are freely distributed through our website. These items serve to assist ministry leaders, volunteers, and parents in implementing our vision and mission in their churches and homes.

Parenting and Family Discipleship

We have produced various materials and training resources designed to help parents disciple their children. These include booklets, video presentations, family devotionals, children's books, articles, and other recommended resources. Our curricula include take-home pages to help parents apply what is taught in the classroom to their child's daily experience in order to nurture faith.

Bible Memory

Our Fighter Verses™ Bible memory program encourages and equips the church, families, and individuals in the spiritual discipline of Bible memory. The 260 Fighter Verses passages have been uniquely selected for their ability to arm Christians to fight the good fight of faith by focusing on God's promises, His character and worth, killing sin, and hoping in God through the gospel. The 76 shorter Foundation Verses help toddlers and pre-readers lay a firm biblical foundation for life.

For more information on any of these resources and training materials, please contact us.

Truth78.org • info@Truth78.org
(877) 400-1414

GROWING IN THE WORD SERIES

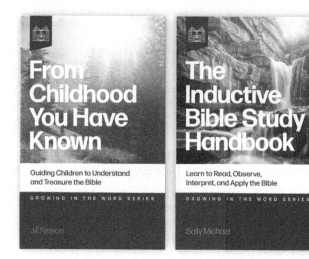

God has given us in the Bible a book like no other, and we have been given the great responsibility and privilege to pass its life-giving truth to the next generation. The Growing in the Word Series aims to inspire and equip the church and home to teach the next generation to read and study the Bible, pray for understanding and a right heart, and apply what they learn to their daily lives.

Resources in this series provide an introduction to the Bible, its message, and use; a reading plan; help with Bible memory and Scripture-focused prayer; age-appropriate training toward biblical literacy; and inductive Bible study tools to help children and youth learn to read, observe, interpret, and apply the Bible to their everyday lives.

Help the children and youth in your home and church come to know and love God's Word and, more importantly, the God who reveals Himself through His Word. Their very life and eternal joy depend upon it!

The following booklets are included in the Growing in the Word Series:

- **From Childhood You Have Known:**
  Guiding Children to Understand and Treasure the Bible
- **The Inductive Bible Study Handbook:**
  Learn to Read, Observe, Interpret, and Apply the Bible
- **Meeting God in His Word:**
  A Guide to Bible Reading and Prayer for Children

Family Discipleship Collection

Inspiration and practical help for teaching and discipling children

- A Father's Guide to Blessing His Children

- Big, Bold, Biblical Prayers for the Next Generation

- Children and the Worship Service

- Dedicated to the Lord: Five Parental Promises for the Faithful Discipleship of Children

- Discipleship through Doctrinal Teaching & Catechism

- Established in the Faith: A Discipleship Guide for Discerning and Affirming a Young Person's Faith

- Helping Children to Understand the Gospel

- Mothers: Disciplers of the Next Generations

- Praying for the Next Generation

- Utter Dependency on God, Through Prayer

Truth78.org/family-discipleship-collection

Zealous

Vision and framework for the discipleship of the next generation.

The next generation needs parents, teachers, and church leaders who are zealous for their discipleship. But where does zeal come from and what does it look like day today?

In *Zealous*, long-time pastor and Truth78 Executive Director, David Michael describes a fervor and diligence born out of a passion for God and His glory and presents seven commitments that provide a vision and framework for your discipleship of the next generation...so that they might set their hope in God (Psalm 78:1-8).

Truth78.org/zealous

A Guide to Growing Zeal for the Discipleship of the Next Generations

Apply the 7 commitments in your church and home

How can you make a vision for the discipleship of the next generations a reality for the children and youth growing up in your home and church? This guide offers practical application of the vision and framework presented in *Zealous*. Find next-step opportunities for each of the seven commitments for children's discipleship in this free PDF.

Truth78.org/grow-zeal

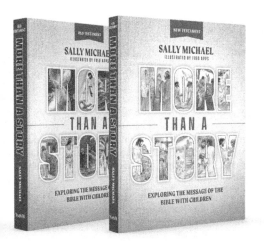

More Than a Story

Introduce children to a glorious God.

More Than a Story takes children (ages 6-12) on a chronological journey through the Bible with a God-centered, gospel-focused, discipleship-oriented, theologically grounded perspective.

Old Testament and New Testament volumes are available individually or as a bundle.

Truth78.org/more-than-a-story

Making HIM Known books

A series of books to teach children about the character and worth of God.

These illustrated family devotionals provide a way for the entire family to learn about our great God and His Word. Each chapter of these read-to and read-along books for elementary-age children ends with personal application and activities and is enhanced by full-color illustrations.

Each book is adapted from a Truth78 curriculum.

Truth78.org/making-him-known-series

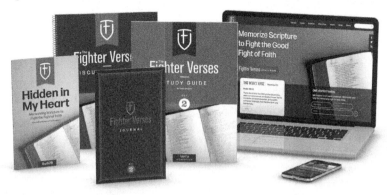

- **FighterVerses.com**—Provides an overview of the Fighter Verses program and its application for individual, family, and church use; includes weekly devotional blog, memory tools, and verse charts.

- **Fighter Verses App**—Portable encouragement with quizzes, songs, study, and review help. Includes additional Bible translations and multiple languages. Available from Apple, Google Play, and Amazon.

- *Hidden in My Heart*—A booklet to equip individual Christians, families, and whole churches to memorize Scripture.

- **Fighter Verses Studies**—Provide deeper study of the weekly Fighter Verses passages.

Ideal for family and classroom use. Leader guides, participant guides, and coloring books for children available for verse sets one and two.

- **Fighter Verses Journal**—Includes a year's worth of memory verses with room for notes and written prayers. Available for sets one and two.

- **Foundation Verses Cards, Visuals, and Coloring Book**—Seventy-six short passages with illustrations to help toddlers and pre-readers lay a firm biblical foundation for life.

- **Memory Cards**—For those who prefer pre-printed paper cards.

FighterVerses.com

Good News of Great Joy products are simple Advent resources to help your family stop and reflect on the true meaning of Christmas, marvel at the providential events surrounding the birth of Jesus, and give thanks for God's provision of the One who has given us "the right to become children of God."

Good News of Great Joy resources include an Advent calendar, a children's book, and a coloring book.

These simple-to-use, reusable resources can become part of your family tradition as you remember together the birth of our Savior and the salvation He obtained for those who are trusting in Him.

Truth78.org/advent

Made in the USA
Coppell, TX
23 August 2023

20711304R00031